Advance praise for the first edition of *The Five Temptations of a CEO*

"A must-read for all leaders, not just CEOs. Take it from someone who has been tempted. Better than a personal coach."
     —**Boyd Clarke,** president and CEO, The Tom Peters Group

"Pat Lencioni delivers a provocative message: CEOs mainly have themselves to blame when things go wrong. If you're a CEO (or any manager for that matter), do you have the courage to face the blame? Doing so could change your future—for the better."
     —**Dr. Jerry Porras,** coauthor, *Built to Last*; professor Stanford School of Business

"A truly enjoyable story. I found myself immediately trying to decide whether I had fallen victim to the temptations. I think most executives will be able to recognize parts of themselves in this well-written, enlightened book!"
     —**Ellyn McColgan,** president, Fidelity Investments Tax Exempt Services Co.

"What a pleasure! Reading *The Five Temptations of a CEO* was like taking a refreshing look in the mirror and really seeing what was there. There is a little of Andrew O'Brien in all of us and, at times, a lot of him in many of us. What a useful tool this book can be for many CEOs."
     —**Lenny Wilkens,** the winningest coach in NBA history

"This book provides extraordinary insight into the pitfalls that leaders face when they lose sight of the true measure of success—results. This model is required reading for my staff."

    —**Dr. Eric Schmidt**, chairman and CEO, Novell Corporation

"The most fascinating book I have ever read about management. Pat Lencioni thrusts into the psyche of a CEO in an extremely shrewd manner and reveals the vulnerabilities there. I could not help but feel that I was the one being confronted while reading it."

    —**Tadao Kobayashi**, Executive Vice President, American Honda Motor Company

"Lencioni goes right to the core of what is at once simple and profoundly hard to do as a leader: to take actions that are conscious and honest, always. He challenges us to be authentic— at precisely those moments when we are most tempted to act out of ego, vanity, or fear. When I am doing a good job, I'm aware of following the principles he suggests."

    —**Dr. Diane Flannery**, CEO, Juma Ventures

"Leadership is about motivating others to achieve superior results. It demands that individuals rise above the inherent human temptations so clearly articulated in this book. Insightful and entertaining, *The Five Temptations of a CEO* provides a practical construct that will help every general manager become more effective."

    —**Thomas J. Tierney**, Worldwide Managing Partner, Bain & Company

"*The Five Temptations of a CEO* is a powerful book. Powerful in its simplicity, powerful in its honesty, powerful in its humanity. Pat Lencioni is a wise and engaging storyteller who knows from real close up what it takes to survive and thrive in one of the loneliest places on the planet—the boss's office!"

—**Jim Kouzes,** coauthor, *The Leadership Challenge* and *Credibility*; Chairman, Tom Peters Group/Learning Systems

"Outstanding! I've read many management books and this one is great! All managers can learn from this quick-reading, honest, and simple to understand book. It is a must read if you want to improve your executive management skills. I've made a wallet-sized reference card of the five temptations so that I don't stray."

—**Michael Rowe,** President and Chief Operating Officer, New Jersey Nets

"*The Five Temptations* gets to a level of organizational truth in a compelling way. It will change the way we look at our behavior and priorities without feeling guilty. The late-night commute home will never be the same. . . ."

—**Richard A. Moran,** best-selling author, *Never Confuse a Memo with Reality*

"Take it from a confirmed 'business book basher': *The Five Temptations of a CEO* is not singing the same old song. No jargon, no pseudo-science, no strained sound-bites, no tedium—just a percipient parable for those on whom others depend for leadership."

—**Mitch Daniels,** Senior Vice President, Corporate Strategy and Policy, Eli Lilly and Company

"Lencioni understands the subtle but critical challenges that every CEO must ultimately face."
—**Mark Hoffman,** President and CEO, CommerceOne

"Some practical and profound choices for leaders at all levels—in any organization! The fable is a great way to get hooked."
—**Tom Kurtz,** architect, coach, navigator, facilitator for organization breakthrough, Procter and Gamble

"Good CEOs are going to love this book. Bad CEOs will be disturbed by it because they're going to realize that all the problems in the organization start with them."
—**Mark Talucci,** President and CEO, The Sak

"Most of us have succumbed to one or more of the 'temptations' described in this book—but not for long. This book is worthy of the attention of any CEO or manager at any level."
—**Timothy F. Finley,** Chairman and CEO, Jos. A. Bank Clothiers

"A good story that conveys wisdom for all human institutions, certainly including not-for-profits."
—**Brian O'Connell,** Founding President, Independent Sector

"Using a 'novel' format, Lencioni guides not only CEOs, but also all managers, to a more productive way of thinking . . . and acting!"
—**David Chilton,** author, *The Wealthy Barber*

"*The Five Temptations of a CEO* really got me thinking. It made me reexamine my own performance and gave me some insights on how I could do my job better."

—**Jerome L. Dodson,** President, The Parnassus Fund

"Lencioni has found a great way to communicate about the issues we face as leaders. . . . A quick, easy, enjoyable read!"

—**John Stoner,** President and General Manager, True Temper Hardware

"Well, well, well. I am tempted to read it again! Would that make the sixth temptation? I actually read it on vacation and could not put it down. A very clever approach to bringing clarity to the CEO mystique and process. In leading my own initiatives, these concepts were abundantly relevant. I look forward to providing a copy of this to all the CEOs in our portfolio."

—**Rick Patch,** Partner, Sequel Venture Partners

THE FIVE
Temptations
OF A CEO

Also by Patrick Lencioni

Leadership Fables

The Four Obsessions of an Extraordinary Executive

The Five Dysfunctions of a Team

Death by Meeting

Silos, Politics, and Turf Wars

The Three Signs of a Miserable Job

Field Guide

Overcoming the Five Dysfunctions of a Team

THE FIVE
Temptations
OF A CEO

A LEADERSHIP FABLE

· · · · ·

PATRICK LENCIONI

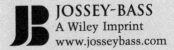

JOSSEY-BASS
A Wiley Imprint
www.josseybass.com

Published by Jossey-Bass
A Wiley Imprint
989 Market Street, San Francisco, CA 94103-1741   www.josseybass.com

Jossey-Bass books and products are available through most bookstores. To contact Jossey-Bass directly call our Customer Care Department within the U.S. at 800-956-7739, outside the U.S. at 317-572-3986, or fax 317-572-4002.

Jossey-Bass also publishes its books in a variety of electronic formats. Some content that appears in print may not be available in electronic books.

Library of Congress Cataloging-in-Publication Data

Lencioni, Patrick M., 1965–
     The five temptations of a CEO: a leadership fable / Patrick M. Lencioni. — 1st ed.
          p. cm.
          ISBN 0-7879-4433-5 (acid-free paper)
          I. Title.
PS3562.E479 F5 1998
813'.54—ddc21   98–9097

Commemorative edition: 978-0-470-26758-5

Printed in the United States of America
FIRST EDITION
HB Printing   10 9 8 7 6 5 4 3

Contents

TRIBUTE

It's hard to believe that it has been ten years since Patrick Lencioni burst onto the national scene with his best-selling book, *The Five Temptations of a CEO*. I never will forget reading that book for the first time and learning about the five temptations:

- Temptation #1: Choosing status over results
- Temptation #2: Choosing popularity over accountability
- Temptation #3: Choosing certainty over clarity
- Temptation #4: Choosing harmony over conflict
- Temptation #5: Choosing invulnerability over trust

Since this book came out in 1998, Patrick has had even greater success with *The Five Dysfunctions of a Team*, *The*

Three Signs of a Miserable Job, Death by Meeting, Silos Politics and Turf Wars, and *The Four Obsessions of an Extraordinary Executive.* These books have become business classics—and required reading for Orlando Magic employees—and have lifted Patrick to a highly treasured slot as one of America's business gurus. You will not want to miss absorbing the many truths and life lessons that he offers.

I have shared the speaking podium with Patrick on a number of occasions. He's an even better speak than writer, if that is possible. His ability to mesmerize an audience with humor, brutal frankness, and wise counsel makes him a highly sought-after lecturer. I am most impressed, however, with Patrick's people skills. Despite his awesome success and fame, he remains approachable as he is never too busy or distracted to spend time talking with his fans.

I predict that *The Five Temptations of a CEO* will have greater success on the second go-round than on the first. If you missed it before be sure to read it thoroughly and then start applying the valuable lessons to your life immediately. Your success as a CEO is guaranteed to reach the highest levels.

Pat Williams
April 2008

FOREWORD

I must admit that I find it surprisingly difficult to reflect on the last ten years since the publishing of my first book, *The Five Temptations of a CEO*. Some of that is just my personality, but most of it is due to the fact that the last decade for me has been a blur.

In the year that the book was published, my wife gave birth to our first children (twin boys), we bought our first home, and a group of friends and I started a little consulting firm called The Table Group. Unbelievably, the nine years that have followed have been busier than the first one.

Since that time, my family has grown (two more boys), as has our consulting firm. I've been blessed to write five more books. To my surprise, I've also been asked to consult and speak to many wonderful organizations, companies, schools, and of course, churches. And so much of the opportunity I've had is due to the success of my first little book, one that was largely an accident.

More than ten years ago, I began consulting to a handful of CEOs from organizations of various sizes and industries. Over time, I began to notice a few consistent behavioral patterns—five actually—that seemed to be causing problems for these leaders, and I did what I do most naturally. I talked about it.

I explained my evolving theory to anyone who was interested, and I learned that people actually thought it made sense. And then one day a client said, "Pat, you should write a book about this." I initially dismissed the idea as flattery, until that person said, "Well, if you don't do it, someone else will." And so I decided to be an author.

Wanting to tap into my interest in screenwriting, I decided to convey my message in the form of a fable. And with the support of my wife and the constant urging of a dear friend, I finally finished the book with generally low expectations that it would ever get published. In fact, my colleagues and I at The Table Group talked about taking the manuscript to Kinko's and making copies to give to prospective clients.

We did, however, decide to submit the manuscript to a few publishers, and to our great surprise, the second one we sent it to decided to take a chance on this unique little fable.

A year after publication, *The Five Temptations* became something of an underground best-seller, which made my publisher, Jossey-Bass, comfortable in allowing me to write another book. A couple years later, as I saw my clients applying my leadership model to groups of people, I decided to write my third and best-selling book to date, *The Five Dysfunctions of a Team*, based largely on the same theory I outlined in *The Five Temptations*. Looking back, I could never have imagined that it would all play out this way.

Some of the questions I've been asked by readers recently are why I think my ideas have been so well received and what I've learned about the model over the past ten years. Two things stand out.

The first was something that Ken Blanchard, the author of *The One Minute Manager*, told me after hearing one of my talks years ago. He approached me backstage and explained to me that the principles behind the five temptations are actually rooted in the Bible. This is something that I've come to understand and appreciate more and more with each passing year.

The other pleasant surprise for me was how readers embraced the simplicity of the book's model. I have always believed that the world has more than enough intelligence and complexity to get along, but that what is really lacking is a compelling, simple explanation of what we already know. Which brings me to one of my favorite quotes from the writer Samuel Johnson: "People need to be reminded more than they need to be instructed."

I think that *The Five Temptations of a CEO*, more than anything, is just a reminder of simple concepts that we already know and have possibly known for a long time. I wrote it for real people in imperfect organizations who are hungry to be better leaders and managers. I am thankful to God for what it all has become, and for letting me be part of it.

Patrick Lencioni
April 2008

INTRODUCTION

Being the chief executive of an organization is one of the most difficult challenges a person can face in a career. But it is not a complicated one.

Some CEOs, especially the struggling ones, might disagree with this statement. They'll tell you their jobs are riddled with complexities and subtleties that make success impossible to predict. If their organizations fail, they may point to a tired list of causes like strategic errors, marketing inadequacies, competitive threats, and technology failures. But these are only symptoms of their troubles.

All chief executives who fail—and most of them do at one time or another—make the same basic mistakes; they succumb to one (or more!) of the five temptations.

If this is true, if a CEO's success hinges on just a few behaviors, then why don't more of them succeed? Why do they keep looking at the same financial statements, product development schedules, and marketing reports in search of a silver bullet? I think Lucille Ball answers this question best.

In an old episode of the *I Love Lucy* show, Ricky comes home to find Lucy crawling around the living room on all fours. When he asks her what she's doing she explains that she has lost her earrings. "You lost your earrings in the living room?" Ricky asks. Lucy replies, "No, I lost them in the bedroom—but the light is so much better out here."

For many CEOs the light is best in places like marketing, strategic planning, and finance, safe havens from the painful darkness of behavioral self-examination. Unfortunately, they find little opportunity for meaningful improvement in these areas.

Even relatively progressive executives often stay in the comfort of their "living rooms," sampling management fads and leadership trends in search of relatively painless remedies for their ills. While some of those remedies appear to work for a while, they eventually leave executives exposed to the same basic issues that caused their problems in the first place, the ones explored in this book.

The tragedy here is that most executives are intuitive enough to understand all this—but many of them struggle to do anything about it. Instead, they unconsciously distract themselves and others from their personal leadership issues by getting overly involved in the details of their businesses, often to the point of creating complexity where it shouldn't exist.

Essentially, what they are doing is putting the success of their organizations in jeopardy because they are unwilling to face—and overcome—the five temptations of a CEO.

*To my mother and father, my wife Laura,
and our newborn sons Matthew and Connor*

THE FIVE Temptations OF A CEO

PART
. . . . .
1

THE
FABLE

CHAPTER

· · · · ·

1

Andrew

Andrew O'Brien hadn't been the last person to leave the offices of Trinity Systems for the past five years. In fact, he hadn't stayed past midnight since taking the job of CEO.

As he stared out the picture window from his office above San Francisco, he wondered how it had come to this.

Tomorrow would be the one-year anniversary of Andrew's promotion. It would also be the first board meeting in which he would be accountable for the results of an entire fiscal year. Those results, as he had grown accustomed to saying, were "unspectacular at best."

But the results didn't bother Andrew as much as his state of mind did. Lately, he wasn't comfortable walking the halls of his company. He didn't feel at ease leading his own executive staff meetings. And certainly he wasn't looking forward to meeting with the board tomorrow. They probably wouldn't be too tough on him, he thought, but they wouldn't be patting him on the back either.

Andrew O'Brien could not deny that he was at a low point in his tenure as CEO, a point he never expected to reach so soon.

And then things got worse.

CHAPTER

· · · · ·

2

BART

Staring out toward the Bay Bridge, Andrew noticed that there were no cars heading east toward Oakland. That seemed odd. Andrew always marveled that traffic filled the city at all hours of the night. He looked over at the clock on his desk and saw that it was 12:02 a.m. Even at this hour there were always cars on the bridge. Traffic never really stopped in San Francisco, short of an earthquake.

Then it hit him.

In his mind's eye, Andrew saw the orange road signs he had been driving by on his way home every night for the past two weeks:

BAY BRIDGE CLOSED FOR REPAIRS
MARCH 4 & 5
MIDNIGHT TO 5:00 A.M.

It hadn't occurred to Andrew that he might need to cross the bridge at this hour. Slowly it dawned on him that he would not be driving home tonight. Unless of course he wanted to go out of his way, across the Golden Gate Bridge and back over the Richmond Bridge and down Interstate 80 to Highway 24 and out toward—forget it. It would cost him more than an hour of driving time, and with at least two hours of work to do before tomorrow's meeting, that didn't seem like a good idea.

On any other night he would just check into one of the full-service hotels near the office, give his clothes to the all-night dry cleaning service, and be ready to go by morning. But tonight Andrew wanted to sleep in his own bed, if only for a few hours. Besides, he was determined to see his wife and kids in the morning. Though he would never admit it, Andrew needed a little moral support.

So he put his papers in his briefcase, grabbed his coat, and headed for the door.

The street below was almost as deserted as the offices above, with the exception of the doorway down the block where the homeless man everyone called Benny lived.

Andrew sometimes pondered Benny's plight to give himself a relative sense of relief when things weren't going well in his life. But tonight it didn't work. He could not escape his obsession with the dreaded board meeting that would begin in just nine hours.

As he walked stiffly toward the Bay Area Rapid Transit station two blocks away, Andrew wondered how long it had been since he'd used public transportation. Had it been eight years? Ten?

Riding the escalator down into the subway terminal, Andrew was surprised to see no one around. The BART station was empty.

Taking a ticket from the machine on the wall, he went to a bench where his train would be arriving and sat down. He was surprised that he didn't feel out of place. *Ten years have gone by fast,* he whispered to himself.

Before he could even take his papers out of his briefcase, the train arrived. As the first few cars sped by him and the train began to slow, Andrew noticed that no one was on board. At least that's what he thought.

CHAPTER

· · · · ·

3

Charlie

Taking the first seat near the door, Andrew suddenly felt exhausted. He had intended to work during the 30-minute ride to the suburbs but found himself wanting to just sit there and stare at the color-coded map of the transit system and ponder the geographic layout of the Bay Area. Anything to take his mind off the board meeting.

Just as the train descended into the darkness of the tunnel that ran beneath the bay and Andrew's eyes began to close, one of the connecting doors behind him opened. He turned and saw an elderly man wearing some sort of uniform step into the car. He appeared to be a janitor of some kind; the name "Charlie" was patched onto the pocket of his gray shirt.

Suddenly Andrew felt uncomfortable. *Should I talk to this man?* he thought. *Certainly he'll expect me to acknowledge him; there's no one else on the train. But what do I say?*

It had come to this for Andrew. He had no problem talking to the television reporter from the Financial Network when the stock dropped six months ago. He was completely comfortable making a presentation to more than two hundred analysts at the marketing conference. But for some unexplainable reason, tonight Andrew was uneasy—even nervous—at the prospect of exchanging middle-of-the-night pleasantries with an old man. And a janitor nonetheless.

Before he could think of something to say, the white-haired man walked by him without saying a word, exited into the next car, and was gone.

Andrew was surprised that, instead of feeling relieved, he felt insulted that the janitor had just ignored him.

But again, the board meeting intruded on his thoughts, and Andrew decided it was time to get to work. As he reached for his briefcase, the lights inside the car flashed, then faded, and the train came to a screeching stop. Sitting alone in the dim light, Andrew wondered if things could possibly get worse, when the door leading into the next car opened.

"Come on," the old man in the janitor suit said. "What are you waiting for?" Then he left.

CHAPTER

. . . . .

4

Contact

At first Andrew didn't move. He just looked at the seat next to him as though he were searching for advice from someone who wasn't there. Then, without a great deal of hesitation, he followed the man into the next car. The janitor was sitting with his back toward the door. Whistling.

Andrew decided the old man was crazy. *Who else would be riding a BART train at 12:30 in the morning and asking strangers to follow them?* he thought to himself. *But then again, who's following this guy around a dark train?*

Maybe it was because he was tired; maybe because he was desperate for something to distract him. For whatever reason, Andrew walked up to the man and took the seat across from him.

Before Andrew could speak, the old man said matter of factly, "The heat in this car is the best on the train. On cool nights like this I prefer coming here to talk."

"To talk about what?" Andrew asked, realizing immediately what a ridiculous question it was. "To talk to whom?" would have made more sense.

But the old man answered without a pause. "Whatever you want to talk about."

Puzzled now, Andrew asked the obvious question: "I'm sorry sir, but do I know you?" He always called strangers "sir," especially older men. Even if they were janitors.

The old man smiled. "Not yet."

Convinced now that the old man was nuts, Andrew's tone turned parental, almost condescending. "So then, you work on the train?"

"Sometimes I do. If that's where I'm needed," the old man said without a hint of pretention. "What do you do for a living?"

Andrew seemed at a loss. "Well, I guess I'm in technology."

"What kind of technology?"

"All kinds really. Everything from calculators to commercial computer systems. I work for a company called Trinity Systems."

"Oh yes, I've heard of that."

Andrew wondered if he was just pretending to know the company.

The old man continued his questioning. "So, you're a technical guy, then?"

Andrew paused, decided to just say yes and leave it at that. Then, for some unknown reason, he suddenly felt the need to tell the old man who he was. "Actually, I'm the CEO. My name is Andrew."

"Well, I'm Charlie. Nice to meet you."

As they shook hands, Andrew noticed that the old man hadn't flinched at the mention of his title. *Does he even know what C-E-O stands for?* Andrew wondered. After an awkward silence, he asked the old man "What exactly do you do?"

Charlie smiled. "Listen, Andrew. We're not here to talk about me. Let's talk about you."

The old man's quirky response almost amused Andrew, but tomorrow's board meeting wouldn't permit it. "Actually, I was going to do some work on the ride home. I've got a big meeting tomorrow, and I have a lot to do still." Andrew immediately felt bad for sounding like he was brushing off the old man, which was basically what he was trying to do.

"Oh, I'm sorry," Charlie said politely. "I'll just leave you alone then. You're obviously very busy." He stood to leave, and Andrew decided to let him go.

Suddenly the lights inside the train flashed off—and then on—and then completely off again. The motionless train was now pitch black.

From the darkness Andrew heard Charlie's voice. "Not to worry, young man." Not more than a second later the old man turned on a flashlight. Andrew wondered how he had it ready so quickly, but he was just glad to have the light, so he didn't ask.

Then, as though he had rehearsed the line before, the old man said, "It looks like we might be here a while. Why don't you tell me what's bothering you?"

Andrew just stared at Charlie for a few seconds. Then, as though he were not completely in control of his own response, he replied, "Okay."

He couldn't believe the word came out of his own mouth. *Am I really going to tell this old man, this janitor, my problems? Am I this desperate? Apparently so, because here I go.* Andrew cleared his throat. "I don't know how much you know about business, but being a CEO is pretty complicated."

"It is?" Charlie seemed surprised. "Tell me about it."

"Well, I don't want to be rude here, Charlie." He paused, searching for the nicest way to say it. "But I'm not sure it would be interesting to you."

Charlie frowned.

At first Andrew thought he had offended the old man. Then Charlie spoke.

Looking around the empty train like a spy, the old man leaned over and whispered: "Now, I don't go around telling just anyone this, Andrew, because I don't want to sound like I'm bragging. But when I was a boy, my father ran a company, and I learned a thing or two from him."

Andrew tried to sound impressed. "You don't say. What kind of company?" He was expecting a hardware store or dry cleaner.

"It was a railroad," Charlie said matter-of-factly. "But that's not the point. My father always said that running a company was running a company, regardless of the type of business."

Andrew wondered if the old man wasn't delusional, but he played along. "He did, did he?"

"Oh yes. And something else he said. Don't take this wrong, Andrew, because I'm sure you're very good at what you do. But my father also said that it wasn't complicated—running a company, I mean. He used to say that 'people make it complicated because they're afraid to look at the simple issues.' Pretty much in those exact words."

Andrew was now beginning to feel annoyed. "Charlie, tell me something. How does the son of a railroad president become a janitor on a BART train?"

To Andrew's surprise, Charlie wasn't hurt by the sharp question. In fact, he seemed to take on a new air of kindness. "Now, Andrew, what in heaven's name does that have to do with your issues? If you don't think I have anything valuable to share with you, just say so. I'll be glad to move on to the next car and find another CEO to talk to."

Andrew was impressed by the old man's self-assuredness. And he smiled as he imagined the old man trying to find someone else on the train to talk to at this hour, no less a CEO. He decided to be charitable.

"So, you think I'm making it too complicated, do you, Charlie?"

Charlie answered the question as though it had been asked with complete sincerity. "I can't say for sure, Andrew, because I'm not sitting in your chair right now. But I can say that being a CEO should be conceptually simple."

He paused for effect.

"Unless, of course, you're failing."

Immediately Andrew's cheeks turned bright red and his ears began to burn. Even in the dim light of his flashlight, Charlie noticed the sudden change in his color and expression.

With a sense of urgency and concern, Charlie asked: "Are you failing, Andrew? Because if you are, then we have to talk. I certainly hope you're not giving in to any of the temptations."

Andrew sat up just a little. "Listen, Charlie. I'm not failing. The company is struggling a little, but there are lots of reasons for that. Certainly I don't consider *myself* to be a failure."

Andrew paused for a few seconds; then he added, "But what do you mean by 'temptations'?"

"I mean that if you *were* failing—and it sounds like you don't think you are, but if you *were*—then you would have to be giving in to one of the five tempations that all CEOs face." He let Andrew think about it before he finished the sentence. "Or, heaven forbid, more than one."

Before Andrew could repeat his question, the lunacy of the situation hit him. *Here I am, sitting on a BART train in the middle of the night, letting myself get upset because an eccentric janitor thinks I might be failing.* He wanted to end the conversation and get back to thinking about the board meeting, but the janitor had piqued his curiosity just enough to make him ask, "Could you just quickly tell me what the five temptations are?"

Charlie paused. "Sit back for a few minutes. I've got some questions to ask you."

Andrew took a deep breath, looked at his watch, and leaned back in his seat.

. . . . .

5

The First Temptation

"Tell me this, Andy. What was the best day of your career?"

Andrew considered asking the old man not to call him Andy, a nickname he'd worked hard to kill since business school, but then decided it wasn't worth the trouble. "What do you mean—"

Charlie held up his hand to interrupt Andrew, like a kind parent. "Try not to make it complicated. Just tell me what your best day was."

Andrew considered it for a few seconds. "I'd have to say the day I was promoted to CEO. One year ago tomorrow."

Charlie seemed disappointed by the answer. Not judgmental. Just disappointed. "Why?"

Andrew was surprised by the question. "Gee, Charlie. Being CEO is a pretty big step in a person's career. I worked for twenty years to get where I am."

Charlie seemed to disregard Andrew's answer. "Okay, then, what about the second-best day?"

Andrew took a breath and described his first promotion to vice president, and about how it was the first time his salary "cracked six figures."

Charlie was slowly nodding his head as though he had figured something out. "Okay, Andy. I don't want to be too critical, but—"

Andrew interrupted. "Feel free to be as critical as you like, Charlie. Everyone else is." He smiled in a tired kind of way.

The old man leaned forward and put his hand on Andrew's knee. "I think you've given in to temptation number one. And it's the toughest one to fix."

As much as he wanted to dismiss it with a laugh, Andrew felt a sense of authenticity in the old man that wouldn't let him discount his advice completely. Not wanting Charlie to sense his concern, he responded jovially: "What is this, Charlie? Right off the bat I'm not fixable?"

Andrew's attempt at humor did not diminish Charlie's concern. "Possibly. Some people are just not cut out to be a CEO."

With less humor now, Andrew asked: "Okay, what makes you think I've given in to temptation number one? What is temptation number one, anyway?"

Charlie paused like a bedside doctor about to give his patient a diagnosis of cancer. "Well, I can't be certain, but it seems to me that you may be more interested in protecting your career status than you are in making sure your company achieves results."

Andrew looked puzzled, so Charlie went on.

"Let's use an example." Charlie looked at the ceiling of the train for a moment. "Okay. Here's one. Think about a politician, maybe even the president of the United States. Imagine that I were to ask him the same question I just asked you. 'Mr. President, what was the biggest day of your career?' What would a great president say?"

Andrew shrugged.

"Or think about the head of a nonprofit agency. Or even the coach of a professional basketball team."

Andrew was growing a little tired of the old man's elusiveness. "What are you getting at, Charlie?"

"Well, imagine the president of the United States saying that the greatest day of his career was election day, or inauguration day." Charlie hesitated, but nothing registered on Andrew's face, so he went on. "Or imagine the head of the nonprofit agency saying that her proudest moment was when she received a grant from the government. Or imagine the basketball coach saying his greatest day was signing a big contract with a team."

Andrew frowned. "To tell you the truth, those sound like pretty realistic answers to me."

"They're *extremely* realistic. And that's the problem."

Andrew still seemed confused, so Charlie lowered his voice

to a gentler level. "You know what my father said when I asked him about the best day of his career?"

Andrew shook his head.

"He said it was a toss-up between the day the railroad opened its first passenger line west of the Mississippi and the day the company first turned a profit."

Charlie sensed that something seemed to be sinking in with Andrew now, so he went on.

"You see, a great president of the United States wouldn't be as proud of being elected as he would of actually accomplishing something. And a nonprofit agency shouldn't feel good about getting funding unless they did something meaningful with the money. And there isn't a great coach alive who would say that his best day was getting hired. Winning games and championships is what great coaching is all about."

Andrew decided to fight Charlie a little. "So you're saying that people shouldn't be proud to reach personal milestones in their careers?"

Charlie smiled. "Of course they can be proud of milestones. But not as proud as they are of actually *doing* something with their status. In fact, great CEOs should be almost overwhelmed by the need to achieve something. That is what drives them. Achievement. Not ego."

Andrew decided to ask a question of his own. "Why couldn't a person be so motivated by his ego that he would drive for results? Lots of CEOs have big egos."

Charlie seemed stumped, but just for a moment. "That's true, I suppose a CEO could be driven by ego." Andrew was relieved to be agreed with for once—until Charlie clarified, "But it wouldn't last for long."

"Why not?"

"Because once a person's ego is initially satisfied, they turn their efforts toward enjoying the fruits of their new status. They work less hours. They worry less about the company's performance than they do about their own level of comfort and status."

Andrew nodded his head just slightly to allow Charlie's point. The janitor pressed on.

"Of course, when the company shows signs of failure and the CEO's status is in jeopardy, then he might work hard again, but not because he's concerned about the company. He's really only concerned about his image."

Charlie then asked a leading question, as politely as he could: "Why is it again that you're working so late tonight? I can't imagine that you usually work these hours."

Andrew responded without making the connection to Charlie's point. "Oh no. I'm usually home by seven. But there's a board meeting tomorrow, and things aren't looking too good."

Suddenly Andrew made the connection. He sat in silence, contemplating the point, and seemed unaware of Charlie's presence.

Deciding it was time to change the subject, Andrew relented. "Okay, Charlie. I can buy this. I can admit that it's sometimes tempting for a CEO to put his career, his status, even his ego a little too high on the list of priorities. That's good advice. I could probably work on that one myself." Andrew felt a sense of charitable satisfaction at conceding the point to Charlie, who didn't seem so crazy anymore.

His satisfaction was short-lived when Charlie explained: "But don't get me wrong. It's very hard to overcome this one. It's part of who you are sometimes. And even if you *are* able to resist the first temptation, there are still four more that can sink you."

The Second Temptation

Andrew took a deep breath. "This is starting to sound pretty negative."

"Not negative. Just difficult. I said before that being a good executive, especially a CEO, is extremely hard. But remember—"

Andrew interrupted sarcastically. "I know. It's not complicated."

"You don't really believe that, do you, Andy?"

"Not yet. But go ahead."

Charlie set the flashlight on the seat next to him so that its light reflected off the white ceiling of the train. "Okay. Let's assume that you are not overly focused on your career, but that you are completely driven by the results of your company. You can still fail if you give in to temptation number two."

"Which is?"

"Wanting to be popular with your direct reports instead of holding them accountable."

Andrew waited to see if Charlie had anything else to say. When he didn't, Andrew remarked, "That's it?"

"What do you mean, 'That's it'?"

"I mean, accountability is the most overused buzzword in business today. Every time something goes wrong, people say that there should be more accountability."

Charlie didn't seem hurt by the dismissal of his theory. Andrew continued. "And popularity. That's something kids talk about in junior high."

Charlie just smiled. "I told you it's simple."

Andrew wanted to move on. With a laugh he said, "Well, I can say that I don't have a problem with accountability *or* popularity. Let's move on to temptation number three."

"Okay. But first let me ask you why you're so sure about this."

With a look of feigned contriteness, Andrew explained. "Well, for starters, last week I fired my head of marketing. I'm not afraid to take action when I have to." He seemed almost proud.

Charlie looked skeptical. "I see."

Andrew was annoyed by the old man's hesitation, but he wanted to know what Charlie was thinking. "You're not convinced."

Charlie responded apologetically. "I'm sorry, Andrew. I just think you're confused about something. Do you mind if I test you on this one?"

"Go ahead."

"Okay. Why exactly did you fire this marketing guy? What's his name?"

"Terry. I fired him because he wasn't getting the job done. He was here for ten months and wasn't cutting it. He came to meetings unprepared. His advertising ideas were stale. He wasn't generating the kind of leads that sales needed." Andrew sounded as if he were trying to convince himself.

Without any sense of accusation, Charlie asked, "So what did you do?"

"I told you. I fired him."

"No, I mean, what did you do along the way? I'm sure you talked to him at some point during those ten months before you fired him."

"Oh, sure. I talked to him about things. But for the most part, I just treated him like anyone else. In fact, I'd have to say that I actually liked Terry better than most of my other direct reports."

"But you saw that he was struggling?"

"Oh yeah. Our head of sales said she wasn't getting the quantity or quality of leads she needed. And none of us thought the advertising was worth a damn."

"What did you say to Terry?"

Andrew thought about the question for a moment. "I don't know. I told him that Janice—she's my head of sales—

wanted more high-quality leads. I mentioned that I liked last year's ads better than his new ones."

"What did he say?"

"That he was still learning the ropes. Which sounded reasonable to me. He was still pretty new."

"And things didn't change?"

"That's right. So I asked him how things were going, and he said that the situation he inherited from the last marketing guy was worse than he had imagined. He said it was going to take longer than expected to turn things around."

"Did you do anything specific at that point? Cut his pay? Withhold a bonus? Anything like that?" Charlie seemed to be rooting for a yes answer.

Andrew frowned. "No. Not giving him a bonus or cutting his pay would have been harsh. He'd just moved his family halfway across the country."

"So I guess you didn't tell him that his job was in jeopardy either?" Charlie knew the answer.

"No way. I didn't want to make him nervous. I figured

things would probably improve with time, and that I shouldn't do anything that might defunctionalize him."

"And then?"

"Three weeks later I fired him."

For a moment, just a moment, Charlie and Andrew stared at one another as they contemplated Andrew's response. And then they started laughing, in a guilty kind of way.

After a few seconds, Charlie asked: "Just like that? You just fired him?"

Trying unsuccessfully to wipe the guilty smile off his face, Andrew defended himself. "No, of course not. Sales were still lagging. Then Terry placed a horrible ad in *USA Today* last month. I started getting calls from board members wondering what was going on in marketing. I decided it was the right thing to do."

"Was he surprised?"

"Oh yeah. I couldn't believe it. I thought he was going to cry for a second there. Which told me something."

"What?"

"That he was out of touch. He should've known that he was in trouble. I mean, we talked about generating more leads at every staff meeting, and nothing seemed to change."

Charlie frowned and squinted as though he were debating whether to say what what was on his mind.

"What's wrong?"

"Andrew." Charlie addressed him by his formal name. "I'm going to be tough on you. Is that alright?"

"Sure." This time Andrew didn't seem to mean it.

With barely a hint of scolding, Charlie asked, "Why didn't you tell Terry that you would let him go if things didn't improve?"

"I already told you, we talked about lead generation at every—"

Charlie interrupted. "Yes, I know. You talked about lead generation. But that's quite different from telling someone that he might lose his job."

Andrew was clearly getting frustrated by Charlie's line of questioning, but the old man went on.

"If you were fired tomorrow by the board, would you be surprised?"

This came too close to home for Andrew, who almost snapped at the old man. "That is totally outrageous. The board is not going to fire me."

The old man held up his hand and dropped his head a bit. "I'm sorry. I didn't mean to say that they actually *are* going to do something like that. It's just—"

Calming down quickly, Andrew interrupted. "I know what you meant, Charlie. I'm sorry, it's just that it's late and I've been under pressure and—"

Andrew stopped talking, as though he had run out of words. He and Charlie sat and stared at the darkness outside the train.

Finally, Andrew broke the silence. "So, what were you saying?"

"It's not important, Andy. I don't want to upset you. Really."

"You're not upsetting me. It's good to get pushed out of my comfort zone from time to time. I read that somewhere."

They laughed.

"Go ahead, Charlie."

"Okay. I was just asking how you would feel if the board was thinking about replacing you. Without telling you."

Andrew now considered the question intellectually. "Well, certainly I wouldn't be happy. But the truth is, it happens all the time. Boards don't give CEOs lots of warning and advice. They aren't the CEO's manager. I see them as having a control function more than anything else."

"That's true. But you *were* Terry's manager."

Andrew rubbed his eyes as he pondered the point. "You know, I have to say that I didn't really see myself as Terry's manager. I don't think I'm Janice's manager, or Phil's, Tom's, Mary's, or anyone else's on my team."

"Why in heaven's name not?"

"Because they're all adults, and they're experts at what they do. Who am I to tell them how to do their jobs?"

Charlie smiled a knowing, parental smile.

Andrew felt Charlie's disapproval, and he finally broke. Speaking more quickly and forcefully than he did before, he explained: "Okay, Charlie. I'll tell you why I never told

Terry that he might lose his job. For one, he's older than me by almost ten years. It feels pretty damn weird telling a guy who reminds you of your uncle that you might fire him. Second, he knows a hell of a lot more about marketing than I do. How was I supposed to second-guess his decisions? My background is in electrical engineering. Three, Terry was one of the few people on my team I could go to and talk about the pressure I was under. He was probably more supportive than anyone on my staff. I didn't want to lose him as a sounding board."

"So you thought that if you told him about your intentions, he might not like you as much, and might not feel like being your confidant anymore?"

Andrew half nodded, so Charlie pressed on.

"You were afraid to be unpopular."

"Come on. I fired the poor guy."

Suddenly Charlie became slightly agitated. "Yes, and now you don't have to deal with him anymore, do you? It's one thing to hold someone accountable for something and come back the next day and deal with him. It's another to fire him and never have to talk to him again."

Stunned, Andrew just sat there digesting his words. Even Charlie was shaken by the directness of his own tone. "I'm sorry, it's just that—"

In a daze, Andrew interrupted, as though he hadn't even heard the beginning of Charlie's apology. "You know something, Charlie? As horrible as it sounds, I know plenty of CEOs who do the same thing. It's not as cut-and-dry as you make it sound. There are all kinds of personal dynamics and context to deal with."

Calmly, Charlie responded. "Yes, it's very common. But that's because they don't understand the difference between holding someone accountable and deciding to fire them."

Andrew shrugged as though he were giving up, so Charlie tried a new approach.

"Andy, in seventeen years as CEO of the railroad, do you know how many people my father fired?"

Andrew shook his head. Charlie held up his hand with five fingers extended.

Andrew rolled his eyes. "I don't mean to be disrespectful to your father, but that's ridiculous. Was he running a railroad or a charity?"

"You're misunderstanding me. I said my father only *fired* five people. But I didn't say how many people left the company because they couldn't perform."

"What do you mean?"

"I mean my father was a fanatic about performance. People who worked for him knew that they either produced or were gone."

"So how come he didn't fire more people?"

"Because he told them what he expected and reminded them of those expectations constantly. When they failed, he made the consequences clear, whether it was financial or otherwise. Eventually, if a person couldn't find a way to improve, they would just leave."

Andrew looked skeptical. "What about the five people he *did* fire?"

"Two of them violated company rules. My father never told me what they did. The other three were people who just couldn't come to terms with their failures. They couldn't bring themselves to leave, so my father did it for them."

For the first time, Andrew was beginning to like Charlie's father. "Your dad sounds pretty tough."

"Yeah, I guess he was tough. But it crushed him to fire those people. Still, he had no choice."

"Come on, sure he had a choice."

"Not in his mind. If he had let those five stay, he would have been letting people down."

"You mean shareholders."

"No. My father felt a sense of duty toward all the people who left on their own when they couldn't perform. He felt like he had to uphold the standards they held themselves to."

Charlie paused. Andrew could tell the old man was thinking about his father.

Andrew paid his respects: "Your father sounds like a wise man, Charlie. I bet he was a great CEO."

Charlie nodded.

Andrew continued. "Now don't take this wrong, but I'd have to say that business today is a little more complicated than it was back then."

Charlie wasn't upset by the comment. "Why do you say that?"

"Where should I start? There's global competition, technology changes, more regulations than ever before. It's just complicated. Back then they had government protection. Cheap labor. Things are harder today."

"So, this situation with Terry. You don't suppose that my father's approach would have worked?"

Andrew pretended to consider the question. "To be honest, probably not."

"Why not?"

"It's like I said before. I wouldn't have known specifically what to hold him accountable for. I would have been guessing. This industry is complex, and I can't pretend to know more about marketing than Terry does. He's the expert."

Charlie shifted in his chair and leaned forward. "So let me get this straight. It's not fair to hold a guy accountable for something specific because you aren't an expert in his field. But it's fair to fire him without warning when he doesn't meet your expectations? Do I have that right?"

Andrew didn't know what to say. "It isn't that simple."

"It *is* that simple. That's the point. It's not supposed to be complicated. You make it complicated because you're not facing your own issues."

At this point Andrew felt challenged by the old man. "Okay, Charlie. Why do you think an intelligent person with an MBA would want to be popular rather than hold someone accountable for their job?"

"Ah, that brings us to temptation number three."

CHAPTER

· · · · ·

7

The Third Temptation

The lights on the train flashed on, off, and then on again, and the train began to move forward slowly.

Andrew sighed. "Finally." He checked his watch and immediately realized that he might have made Charlie feel that he wanted to end the conversation, which wasn't his intention at all. So he encouraged the old man to continue.

"What is temptation number three, Charlie?"

Charlie wasn't convinced that he really wanted to know. "I don't want to bore you with any of this. I better let you get back to your work."

Andrew responded kindly, and just a little patronizingly. "Don't stop now, Charlie. I need to know why I don't feel comfortable holding people accountable. You can't just leave me here with the first two temptations. I need to know the other three."

Charlie sensed the condescension in Andrew's voice, so he said politely, "I'm sure you'll be fine. It sounds like you've got it figured out for yourself."

But Andrew was more curious than he wanted to admit. The prospect of not finding out the rest of the old man's advice was troubling. In a more genuine tone he said, "I'd really like to hear what you have to say."

Charlie paused. "Okay. If I'm not troubling you too much."

"Not at all. What is temptation number three?"

"It's the temptation to ensure that your decisions are correct."

Andrew looked confused, so Charlie clarified.

"It's the temptation to choose certainty over clarity. Some executives fear being wrong so much that they wait until they're absolutely certain about something before they make a decision. That makes it impossible to hold people accountable."

"I'm not sure I'm following you."

"It's simple. You can't hold people accountable for things that aren't clear. If you're unwilling to make decisions with limited information, you can't achieve clarity."

"Okay. I get it. But what kind of things are you talking about?"

"Simple things. Important things. Like why the company is in business. Its goals. The roles and responsibilities of people in the organization to meet those goals. The consequences for success and failure. All that stuff."

Andrew nodded. "Vision, mission, values, goals. Business-school stuff. Don't take this wrong, Charlie, but none of this is new."

"Of course not. People talk about this all the time." Charlie paused for effect. "So then, what is your vision of the future for Trinity?"

Andrew frowned and scratched his shoulder like a kid trying to avoid a scolding.

Charlie was surprised. "Don't you know?"

"Yeah, it's just we're having a hard time settling on the right way to explain it. In fact, we'll probably discuss it again tomorrow at the board meeting."

"How long have you been working on this?"

Andrew squirmed a little, trying to come up with an answer, so Charlie prompted him. "A month? Two?"

Andrew finally admitted: "Eight months."

Charlie was genuinely surprised. "Eight months?! What in God's name is taking so long?"

"Well, it's just that the market is changing and we're trying to figure out whether our current business is going to be able to sustain—"

Charlie interrupted. "I'm sorry, Andy, but this is ridiculous. And please excuse me for saying this, because I haven't known you very long, but not having a vision is no one's fault but your own."

The truth hit Andrew hard. He wanted to defend himself, but before he could get the words out of his mouth, Charlie beat him to it. "And don't tell me it's more complicated than that."

Andrew deflated in his seat as Charlie took away his only response. He was beginning to feel overwhelmed, and his eyes were glazing over. "It's not that simple."

Charlie leaned forward. "Stay with me here, Andy. I'm going to ask you some tough questions."

"You mean they haven't been tough so far?"

Charlie ignored the humor. "Are you up to this?"

Slowly, Andrew sat up, like one of his sons about to be grounded. "Yeah. Go ahead."

"Okay. What is preventing you from coming to some conclusions on something as big and important as your company's vision?"

"I wish I knew."

"You *do* know, Andy. It's just that you have to admit it to yourself. Face your fears. You must have some idea about what the future of your company should look like."

"Sure I do."

"So why haven't you put it on paper, announced it to the company, and used it to guide the decisions you make?"

After a long pause, Andrew slowly, quietly responded, "Because I'm not sure it's right yet."

Silence. The sentence just hung there, until Charlie asked "Were you ever in the military?"

He shook his head.

"Well, in the military, they teach you that any decision is better than no decision."

"I've heard that before, but this is different."

"You're right. This is completely different. No one's lives are on the line in your company."

Andrew struggled for relief. "I'll tell you what, Charlie. I think the whole vision, mission thing is overrated."

"I agree. I think that having a great vision and mission is only important if you know how to execute. I'll take a well-executing company over a visionary one any day."

"Exactly." Andrew thought he had found relief when Charlie agreed with him. Until the old man asked the next question.

"So, what are your goals for the next three months?"

"Me personally?"

"No. The company. What needs to get done so that you can say it was a successful period?"

"We've got to make more money. We need to grow our market share."

"By how much? And what needs to happen for you to get there?"

Andrew was frustrated to the point of anger now. "I'll tell you what, Charlie. I've just about had it with your folksy preaching. It's easy for you to ask all these questions in a vacuum, and it's easy to be smug about—"

Charlie looked hurt by the remark, but he interrupted Andrew kindly. "Do you think I'm being smug?"

"No, it's just that it's too easy to sit outside and drill me here like an attorney, because there are no easy answers."

For the first time, Charlie became emotional. "There aren't supposed to be easy answers, Andy. That's why you get paid so much. But you have to come up with answers. Otherwise, there is no accountability. And without accountability, results are a matter of luck." He paused for a breath, but couldn't quite calm himself enough to stop from asking the next question. "How could you fire Terry and not know what he should have been doing?"

Andrew just sat there shaking his head.

Charlie moved forward in his seat. "I think you're afraid to be criticized. To look bad."

"No one likes to look bad."

"Of course they don't. But the price for you is too high. You're driving your company into the ground, whether the board of directors realizes it or not."

That came out of nowhere to Andrew, and he shouted at Charlie. "I'm not afraid to be criticized! And I'm not driving the company—"

Charlie interrupted Andrew and shouted back at him. "Then where is your vision, Andy? Where are your goals? Make a darn call on something. What are you waiting for?"

Suddenly the train ground to a halt, and the lights flickered and went out again. The two angry men just sat there in the dark for five minutes. A full five minutes.

Then the flashlight went on, but this time Andrew was holding it. Calmly, he spoke. "So what is my problem here, Charlie?"

Charlie responded kindly, barely above a whisper. "Let me tell you something. From what I can tell, many CEOs have the same problems. They finally get the job they've always wanted, and they become afraid to lose their status. Or they don't want to hold people accountable because they're afraid to be unpopular. And even if they aren't afraid to be unpopular, they don't hold people accountable because they haven't bothered to be clear about what they expect from people because—"

Andrew finished the rest of the lesson. "Because they're afraid to be wrong."

"Exactly." Charlie let Andrew digest the message. Then: "My father used to say that there were three words which were the most powerful thing a CEO could say. Do you know what those are?"

Andrew shook his head.

"'I-WAS-WRONG.' But the thing is, he didn't say those words apologetically. He said them like he was proud of them. He knew that if he couldn't be comfortable being wrong, he wouldn't make tough decisions with limited information."

Andrew was now ready for help. "So he must have made a lot of bad decisions."

"Sure he did. And he owned those decisions. But he never felt guilty about them because he knew that you can't move forward in the face of uncertainty if you aren't willing to make mistakes. And gradually, he made fewer and fewer mistakes. In fact, people said he developed an amazing ability to make good decisions without enough information. They thought he was really smart."

Partly out of respect, partly because he meant it, Andrew offered, "He seems pretty smart to me."

Charlie smiled. "As much as I hate to say it, my father wasn't really any more intelligent than the average person. In fact, he used to say that the key to his success was hiring people who were smarter than him."

"So how did he learn to make such great decisions?"

"Well, he avoided temptation number four."

CHAPTER

· · · · ·

8

The Fourth Temptation

N ow Andrew was genuinely interested in Charlie's
advice, and he felt no reason to hide it.

"Okay. What's temptation number four?"

"It's the temptation to—"

Charlie was interrupted by the sound of one of the connecting doors opening. Andrew spun around in his seat to
see who it was.

Standing in the door was a tall man wearing a suit and hat.
He addressed Charlie politely.

"Excuse me. Are you coming back? It's been quite a while."

Charlie slapped himself on the forehead. "Oh, my. I *have* been gone quite a while haven't I? I'm so sorry."

Andrew was very confused.

The Tall Man spoke again. "I thought you might have left."

Charlie seemed almost hurt. "Oh no. I wouldn't do that. It's just that I started having such an interesting conversation with Andy here that I lost track of the time."

Charlie seemed perplexed by the dilemma on his hands. Then something occurred to him.

"Andy, why don't you come join us? No sense in me running back and forth keeping everyone waiting."

Before Andrew could respond, the Tall Man said, "Hey Charlie, the heat in here is better than the other car."

"Yes, I know, it's the best on the train."

The Tall Man turned back toward the door to leave. Charlie and Andrew followed him.

Andrew was just about to stop and ask Charlie what was

going on, but something told him he wasn't supposed to ask. Somehow, the situation was just too preposterous for a simple question like Where are we going? or Who is this guy? Andrew decided that he would find out in due time.

Charlie let Andrew walk ahead of him, which offered Andrew a chance to check out the Tall Man from ten feet behind as they traveled the length of seven train cars.

His suit was in good condition but seemed out of style to Andrew. His shoes, although new, reminded Andrew of something he had once dragged out of his grandfather's closet.

The Tall Man entered the seventh car and stopped. Andrew heard voices inside, so he hesitated.

"Go ahead," Charlie encouraged him. "They won't bite."

"They?" Andrew replied. But that's all he could get out before Charlie nudged him into the next car.

Immediately he noticed that there were two other men in the car, in addition to the Tall Man. Both were in their late forties or early fifties. They were sitting in the middle section of the train, facing one another, involved in an animated conversation. One was bald. The other wore a stylish, double-breasted suit with pinstripes.

The Tall Man asked for their attention. "Excuse me, gentlemen. This is Andy." He turned to Andrew. "It's Andy, right?"

Andrew nodded.

Charlie chimed in. "Andy is the CEO of Trinity Systems, the technology company. He and I lost track of time."

Neither of the men seemed at all surprised to see Andrew, and like Charlie they didn't react to his title.

The Stylish Man spoke first. "How far did you guys get, Charlie?"

Andrew was confused, and began to feel a sense of nervousness—almost panic. *What's going on here?* he thought, suddenly wondering if this were some sort of scam or setup.

Charlie looked at Andrew, frowning in thought. "How far did we get?" But before Andrew could even grasp the point of the question, Charlie remembered. "Oh, yes. We were just starting temptation number four."

The three men acknowledged temptation number four with nods and ahhs and smiles.

The Tall Man spoke. "Number four is my big challenge."

Andrew began to feel he was in the midst of an episode of *The Twilight Zone*. And then suddenly his concern about the strange situation faded a little as he again became curious about the next temptation.

"What is temptation number four?"

He directed the question at the Tall Man, who looked toward Charlie as if to ask permission. Charlie smiled and nodded, so the Tall Man spoke.

"Have a seat, and I'll explain it to you."

Charlie, Andrew, and the Tall Man sat down.

Taking off his hat, the Tall Man spoke. "Temptation four is the desire for harmony."

Without knowing why, Andrew suddenly felt comfortable with these men. "I don't understand. What does harmony have to do with clarity and good decisions?"

The Bald Man spoke for the first time. "From the perspective of a person who doesn't have a problem with temptation number four"—the others laughed—"let me explain."

All attention shifted toward the Bald Man.

"Answer a question for me, Andy. What is the opposite of harmony?"

Andrew thought for a moment. "I don't know; discord?"

"Discord. Disagreement. Conflict. Any of those will do. The point is, it's natural for human beings to want harmony." He paused. "But harmony is like cancer to good decision making."

Andrew seemed lost, so the Bald Man continued.

"You see, the only way to come to a good decision quickly is to suck all of the honest opinions out of people efficiently. There are two ways to do that."

The Bald Man held up a finger to show that he was explaining the first way. "One, you can put nice processes in place to massage opinions out of people—focus groups, brainstorming sessions, democratic voting." He held up a second finger. "Or two, you can do it in a messy way."

The Tall Man jumped in. "Messy means using conflict. But not bad conflict. We're talking about productive ideological conflict. From the outside, they look the same, but they're very different."

Andrew was starting to grasp their point, but something troubled him. "But isn't that the same as temptation two?"

The others looked confused, so Andrew explained himself. "Temptation number two is the one where you want to be popular with people instead—"

The Stylish Man interrupted. "Instead of holding them accountable. Yes, we know about temptation number two."

"Right, I guess you do. Anyway, isn't wanting to be popular pretty much the same thing as wanting harmony?"

The Bald Man seemed to understand Andrew now. "I see where you're confused. Temptation two is about not wanting to be rejected, as a person. It's about judging yourself by what other people think of you."

The Stylish Man spoke next. "You're confusing the fear of being unpopular with the fear of your group being in conflict with one another."

"But—"

Before Andrew could even begin the sentence, Charlie interrupted him. "No, we're not splitting hairs here, Andy. There is a big difference."

The Tall Man explained. "For instance, I don't have a problem holding people accountable for things, as long as we all agree what those things are. But sometimes I have a hard time deciding what to hold them accountable for, because we make decisions that don't feel right."

Andrew turned to Charlie. "You said your father almost always made good decisions."

"That's right. Because he almost never made a decision without having the full benefit of everyone's ideas."

The Tall Man became excited. "Right. And that's where I fall down. I don't like it when people challenge one another. I try to steer them away from passionate, heated conversations because I'm afraid that someone is going to come out of it getting hurt, or looking bad."

"I don't have that problem." The Bald Man's comment brought out laughter in his colleagues.

"Why is that?" Andrew asked.

"I don't know. I suppose it has something to do with the way I was raised. My brothers and I fought and argued about things all the time, and ten minutes later everything was fine. I guess I learned that there was never any permanent damage."

The Stylish Man added: "Me too. I've never had a problem with allowing people to get into it during meetings. In fact, if no one gets a little pushed out of shape during a meeting, I feel like we probably didn't put all our issues on the table."

Andrew persisted. "I still think that if you have a problem with temptation two, you'll struggle with temptation four."

The Stylish Man responded. "That's sometimes the case. But take me, for example. I love conflict. I can jump up and down on a table, and my people don't hesitate to get in my face about things whenever they feel the need. So we get real clear about what we need to do and about what we're accountable for. It's right out there in front of us."

The Tall Man and the Bald Man began to laugh.

"What's so funny?" Andrew wondered out loud.

The Stylish Man explained. "They're laughing at one of my weaknesses. You see, I sometimes give in to temptation number two; I let people off the hook."

"How so?"

"Well, when one of my people comes to me and tells me that they couldn't meet a deliverable or finish a project on time, I always ask them why. And I'll be damned if most of the time they don't have a pretty good reason." He pauses. "And so I let them off every once in a while."

The Bald Man and the Tall Man objected in unison: "Every once in a while?"

"Alright, alright. I do it way too much. I guess for all of my ranting and raving, I'm pretty soft about things. Too much empathy or something. In fact, I do the same thing with my kids. I'll holler at them and we'll have some pretty passionate discussions, if you know what I mean."

They laughed.

"But then I can't bring myself to actually punish them."

Andrew was beginning to like the Stylish Man. "That doesn't sound like such a bad thing to me."

Suddenly the Stylish Man became adamant. "It's a horrible thing. Horrible."

Andrew was shocked, but he let the Stylish Man continue.

"I lose credibility with people. I seem inconsistent and unfair to them. The next time I need someone to actually deliver on something, they're not sure how serious I am about it. And the funny thing is, do you know why I have this problem?" He paused. "Because I want them to like me."

Andrew asked, "Does it work?"

"You mean, 'Do they like me?' I guess so, but they don't respect me as much as they would if I were consistent. And without respect. . . ." He didn't have to finish the sentence. Andrew was already nodding.

The Tall Man completed the lesson. "But *my* problem isn't that I need to be popular. It's just that I don't feel completely right about holding people accountable, because even though I made a clear decision about what they're accountable for, I know in my heart that they haven't really bought into it. And you know why?"

Andrew shook his head.

"Because I don't let them air their opinions enough. I stifle their arguments before they have a chance to get clear on things. I just don't like conflict."

Andrew added, "And so your decisions aren't based on all the information that your people have to offer."

They all nodded. Andrew was beginning to grasp it all, though he still seemed a little confused, overwhelmed.

Charlie decided to challenge his pupil. "Why don't you give it a shot, Andy?"

"Give what a shot?"

"The temptations. See if you can remember the first four."

Andrew looked around at the four strangers. Before he accepted Charlie's challenge, he asked the unthinkable question: "Who are you guys?"

The Bald Man answered. "We're like you. We're people who've faced these same temptations. But we're not here to talk about us."

Charlie agreed. "That's right, Andy. See if you can remember the temptations."

Andrew looked into his reflection in the window as if he were trying to decide whether he could do it. "Alright, let's see. The first temptation—the one I struggle with the most, as far as I can tell—is the temptation to focus on my career and my status above my focus on the company's results. That makes me complacent and unfocused, and causes results to slip."

Andrew noticed that the four men were nodding at him, except it seemed that they were not so much acknowledging his correct response as confirming his tendency for temptation number one. He shrugged it off and went on with his quiz.

"Okay, even if I were able to overcome temptation number one, I might still get unspectacular results if I give in to temptation number two."

Charlie prompted: "Which is?"

"The need to be liked and popular with my staff, at the expense of holding them accountable. That's your problem, right?" He motioned toward the Stylish Man, who nodded.

"And even when we are not overly concerned about being liked by our people, we fail to hold them accountable because—wait a minute," he paused for a few seconds, "because we don't feel like it's fair to hold them accountable. And that has something to do with temptation number three, which I can't quite remember."

The Bald Man helped him out: "Decisions."

"Right. Clarity. We don't feel it's fair because we don't like to decide things without perfect information. We let things hang there ambiguously, without making clear and timely decisions, because we don't want to be wrong. So we wait, and we wait, and in the meantime, someone has to take the blame for things being—"

The Stylish Man finished the sentence: "Unspectacular."

Andrew smiled. "Right. And so someone might get embarrassed or demoted or fired, even though no one had the guts to tell them what was expected of them. But even when they do have the guts to make things clear, sometimes they fail to make good decisions and achieve buy-in around their clarity because of temptation number four: the desire for harmony."

The Tall Man raised his hand to claim this particular temptation.

Andrew acknowledged him with a smile and went on. "They're afraid to entertain conflict, to put their ideas on the line where they might get challenged. So they don't benefit from the various opinions and ideas of their people. And I suppose that is the root cause of all the confusion, the fear of, what did you call it, productive ideological conflict?"

Charlie smiled and nodded his approval. "Yes. But that is not the root of all this. The root is the fifth temptation."

Just as he finished the sentence, the train began to slow. At once, Charlie, the Bald Man, the Stylish Man, and the Tall Man looked at their watches, stood, and began to collect their belongings. The Stylish Man had an antique briefcase that must have cost a fortune, Andrew thought.

And then it dawned on him: *they're not going to tell me temptation number five.*

The Fifth Temptation

As the train came to a halt, the four men swayed in unison and reached for the overhead bar. Andrew would have found this odd picture amusing were he not so desperate for the conclusion of Charlie's advice.

"You guys aren't serious. You're not going to just stop right there?"

Only Charlie answered. "It's time for us to go, Andy."

The four men moved toward the door, but Andrew stepped in front of it to block them. First the Tall Man, then the Bald

Man, and finally the Stylish Man stepped around Andrew carefully, nodding their heads or tipping their hats to him as they passed.

As Charlie approached, Andrew held out his hand to stop him. With a sense of desperation he said: "Just tell me what it is, Charlie. You don't need to ask me any leading questions or tell me any more boring stories about your father. Just give me the final temptation."

For the first time in the evening, Charlie looked deeply hurt. Andrew apologized immediately.

"I'm sorry. But you can't just leave me hanging."

Charlie took a breath. "Come with me."

Charlie exited the train as Andrew turned toward the seat where his briefcase was. At that moment he heard the hydraulic doors preparing to close. Andrew knew that he would not be able to get out of the train if he went back for his case. He ran to the door and leapt from the train just as the doors closed.

Watching the train carry his briefcase into the next tunnel, Andrew rubbed his eyes and smiled at the crazy night he was having. He turned around to an empty terminal. Everyone was gone, including Charlie.

Desperate again, Andrew ran to the escalator and up toward the street exit. Once outside, he looked up and down the street and saw no sign of Charlie.

Then he heard a voice behind him.

"Over here."

Completely startled, Andrew jerked around and saw Charlie sitting on a bus stop bench. "Oh my God!"

"What's the matter, Andy?"

"What's the matter? I'll tell you what's the matter. First I thought you ditched me. Then you scare me to death."

Charlie was calm, concerned. "No. I mean, what's the matter with you, in general? Why are you so desperate?"

Andrew sighed, walked over to the bench, and sat down next to Charlie. After a few moments, he dropped his head into his hands and spoke.

"For the first time in my career I think I'm drowning. And I feel like I'm pulling people down with me just to keep my head above water."

Charlie said nothing. Andrew continued.

"I've always been able to turn things up a notch when I needed to, but this doesn't seem to be about turning it up at all."

Charlie asked, "What's it about?"

"I don't know. It's like an impossible balancing act, with everything constantly moving. So many subtleties. So many details. Too much stuff. All the stuff."

Charlie patted Andrew on the back. "Let me tell you about temptation number five."

Andrew sat up and took a deep breath. "Okay. Fire away."

"My father—it's alright if I talk about my father, isn't it?"

"Sure, Charlie. I was being a jerk. Your father's stories aren't boring. They're just painful. Go ahead."

"Well, my father wasn't the kind of man to brag, but he did brag about one thing."

"What?"

"He bragged about the people who worked for him. He'd get unusually emotional when he talked about the people on his staff."

Charlie smiled as he thought about it.

"And I remember that he always said he trusted his people with his career." Charlie paused, then asked, "Can you say that?"

Andrew shook his head without hesitating. "Not even close. Some of those people probably wouldn't care one way or the other if I stepped down tomorrow."

Charlie seemed genuinely sad for Andrew. "Why do you suppose?"

Andrew stared off across the empty street. Gradually, he began to shake his head. "I don't know. They're all so focused on their own careers."

"And you?"

"I don't know, Charlie. I guess I'm as concerned about my career as the next guy. But I don't think I'm any worse."

"I'm not asking you that. I was wondering if they could trust you with their careers?"

Andrew stared out across the empty street again. "I don't want to sound like I don't care, but I don't think it's my job to hold these people's careers in my hand."

"That's not the point, Andy. All of this is about trust. It's about risking and building trust. And before they trust you, you have to trust them. You have to be vulnerable."

"Wait a second. What does that have to do with conflict?"

"Well, why do you suppose people are afraid of conflict?"

Andrew shrugged. "I guess they're not used to it. Or their feelings get hurt easily."

"Maybe. But I think it has a lot to do with trust. People who trust one another aren't worried about holding back their opinions or their passions. They say what they think and know that they aren't going to be vulnerable if they do."

"I don't know, Charlie. I think a little tension between people is good. If you trust one another too much, you get soft. You lose your edge. I don't want my people feeling too comfortable."

"Why in heaven's name not?"

"Because people slack off when they're too comfortable."

Charlie became a little impatient with Andrew now. "Come on, Andy. There's a difference between people being complacent and being trustworthy. You're smarter than that."

"Maybe I'm just not a very trusting person."

"Do you know why people don't trust other people?"

"No. Why?"

"Because they're afraid of getting burned. That's what I mean by vulnerability."

Andrew slowly nodded his head. "Yeah. That's probably right."

"And you know what the best cure for that is?"

Andrew shook his head.

"Opening yourself up to being burned. Sometimes it's even okay to get burned, because you realize it's not fatal."

"So you're telling me that I don't like conflict because I don't trust people, and I don't trust people because I'm afraid of being vulnerable."

Charlie nodded. "Being vulnerable. Being wrong. Being unpopular. Losing your status."

"And you're telling me that great CEOs like your father go around leaving themselves open to people stabbing them in the back?"

"As crazy as it sounds, they do. My father never worried about being vulnerable with his people. He trusted them. That is what allowed them to feel comfortable having healthy, productive conflict. No one worried about getting hurt."

Andrew took a deep breath. "So the root of all this is vulnerability?"

Charlie nodded and checked his watch.

Andrew sighed. "This is getting too touchy-feely for me."

"Touchy-feely? Getting results, holding people accountable, creating clarity for your people, engaging in productive conflict with them? If all those depend ultimately on vulnerability and trust, isn't it worth tolerating just a hint of touchy-feeliness, if that's what you think it is?"

Andrew shrugged. "I don't know."

At that moment, a bus pulled up in front of Andrew and Charlie. "That's my ride." Charlie stood to leave.

Andrew asked his final question. "So how do I get comfortable being vulnerable?"

The bus door opened. Charlie patted Andrew on the shoulder and stepped on board.

"You'll have to figure that one out for yourself, Andy. Give it a try."

The old man smiled as the door closed.

Andrew watched as Charlie greeted the bus driver like an old friend. As the bus pulled away, Andrew stepped off the curb, into the street, and watched it disappear.

The blaring sound of a horn startled him. He turned and saw bright lights—an oncoming bus. He screamed.

Again the horn sounded and again Andrew screamed, waking himself as the train pulled into the Walnut Creek station.

Wiping the sleep from his eyes, Andrew checked his watch. Just twenty minutes had passed since he boarded the train. It always amazed Andrew how much dreaming a person could do in a short period of time.

Grabbing his briefcase, which he was glad to know was still there, Andrew stepped from the train and moved toward the exit of the BART station. The next day's board meeting wasn't weighing on him quite as heavily as it had been a half hour earlier.

CHAPTER

. . . . .

10

The Board Meeting

ndrew O'Brien had never been late to a board meeting in his life. But today, at 9:02 A.M., he sat at his desk and stared out the picture window toward the Bay Bridge.

Any confidence he felt last night on his way home from the BART station had disappeared. The men in his strange dream—Charlie, the Bald Man, the Tall Man, the Stylish Man—could not have seemed less relevant now. Andrew was dreading the next few hours of his life.

The phone on his desk rang, and Andrew hit the speaker button.

"Yes, Joan."

She told him what he already knew: "We're waiting for you."

"I'm on my way."

Andrew took a deep breath and headed for the door.

Because it was the annual board meeting, the room was crowded. The Chairman, a large man with tan skin, sat at the head of the table. Twelve others filled in the rest of the long table. Most were board members, with the exception of Stephen, the CFO; Janice, the head of sales; and Andrew's executive assistant, Joan.

Taking the lone vacant chair at the opposite end of the table from the Chairman, he nodded his hellos to the board members. Then he noticed a face he had never seen, a woman with sharp features and streaks of grey hair. Before he could acknowledge her, the Chairman announced: "Andrew, this is Kathryn Petersen from B&L Securities. I think you've spoken a few times during the conference calls last quarter. She's taking Carl's spot on the board."

Andrew remembered talking to Kathryn, but he had forgotten that she would be at the meeting today.

"It's nice to meet you, Kathryn." Andrew crossed part of the room to shake hands with Kathryn, who didn't say anything but smiled politely.

As Andrew returned to his chair, the Chairman began. "Alright. I think we're all familiar with the financial results for the quarter. I'd say they are—"

Andrew interrupted. "Unspectacular, at best."

The people in the room laughed louder than they needed to, the Chairman loudest of all.

"Right. Anyway, you all received a copy of the quarterly and annual financials in your packets, so you're aware of the details. Rather than make Andrew here drag us through the blood and guts, I thought we could focus on some of the initiatives that are under way for the first part of this year."

Many of the board members nodded their approval at the Chairman's suggestion. Andrew wondered if he was going to get off so easily, hoping desperately that he would. Kathryn wrote something on a pad of paper, and he wondered what it was.

The Chairman continued. "Alright, Andrew. I guess we're going to find out about the executive compensation plan for next year and the customer research that was done last quarter."

Andrew nodded to his CFO, Stephen, who would be reviewing the compensation plan. After an hour of light debate about the merits of stock options versus cash bonuses, he sat down. Kathryn made no comments during the discussion but again wrote a short note on her pad.

Andrew then presented a summary of the customer research, explaining that more work would be needed to confirm that print advertising in business magazines was the answer to their marketing woes. There were polite questions from some members of the board, but not from Kathryn, who again made a few notes on her pad but otherwise seemed disinterested in the conversation.

Lunch was brought in at noon, during which Janice explained the plans for reorganizing the telesales organization. The board members applauded gently at the end of her talk.

During the next two hours the board approved a stock repricing initiative and reviewed a shareholder lawsuit. Andrew handled himself masterfully during these conversations, projecting a sense of confidence and humor. He even surprised himself when he found that he was enjoying the meeting.

By two o'clock, the meeting was losing steam and drawing to a close. The Chairman looked at his watch. "Well, I think we've covered everything on our agenda. If there is nothing else, let's call it a day." He turned to Andrew's assistant. "When is our next meeting, Joan?"

Andrew felt a bizarre sense of relief. Bizarre because it was mixed with a hint of guilt. Nonetheless, he couldn't wait to get out of the room, out of the office, and home. As Joan answered the Chairman's question, board members began stacking their papers and portfolios.

Then Kathryn brought a gradual halt to everyone's exit when she raised her hand, trying to get the Chairman's attention. He smiled at her, amused at her overly polite way of getting the floor. "Yes, Kathryn?"

The noise in the room died down a little.

Kathryn frowned and looked down at the pad of paper in front of her. "I have a few questions before we go."

The other board members stopped packing their things.

"Go ahead, Kathryn. I wasn't sure we were going to hear anything from you."

"Well," she said calmly and seriously, "I don't like to do too much talking at my first board meeting. I usually need a few meetings before I see any patterns that I feel comfortable addressing." The Chairman nodded as Kathryn added, "But not this time."

Now the room was completely silent.

Kathryn looked up. "I have a question."

The Chairman looked at Andrew, who did not move.

Kathryn turned toward Andrew. "What do you expect the first couple quarters of the year to look like, Andrew?" Before he could answer, she clarified her question. "I mean, I know what your projections are, but why do you think the problems you had last year are going to get any better?"

Andrew paused, but for only a moment. "Well, first of all, I expect to hire a head of marketing soon, and having that job filled will be a big boost."

Kathryn continued to wait, so Andrew went on. "And the market should get better this year, and that's going to help us. And finally, we're looking at an acquisition candidate to expand our line of services. Those things will definitely help."

Setting her pen down, Kathryn looked toward the Chairman, who didn't react to Andrew's response. "Okay. I sit on a lot of boards, and you pay me real money to be here, so I'm not going to mince my words." The room froze. "You're in real trouble here."

The Chairman spoke. "Certainly the market is not where it should be, and we'd like to see stronger revenue, but I don't think Andrew's numbers are—"

Kathryn interrupted the Chairman politely but sternly. "I'm not talking about the numbers. I just don't see a sense of urgency."

The Chairman almost frowned. Andrew tried not to react.

"Waiting for the market to turn around is pretty passive. And thinking that hiring a new marketing head is all you need is a poor turnaround plan. He's not going to have an impact for at least a few quarters." She looked through her notes. "Oh, and the acquisition thing. You're having a hard time managing this company. I don't think that buying another company is going to do anything but distract you further."

Kathryn's bluntness silenced the room. Stephen made the first move. "I don't want to sound defensive here, but are you completely familiar with our industry? We're doing much better than most of our competitors."

Kathryn responded. "Yes, I know. I did a little research yesterday, and correct me if I'm wrong, but I think you're the number-three player in an industry of six real competitors. Three of them did much worse than you did, but the other two actually did pretty well. I'd say that puts you in trouble."

She thumbed through her papers but couldn't seem to find what she was looking for. "And if I remember correctly, your revenue actually declined since a year ago. The market grew by 5 percent, which is not much, I admit, but certainly you should be getting your fair share of that growth."

The Chairman tried to avoid any bloodshed. "You're probably right, Kathryn. We need to have a greater sense of urgency around some of these issues, but I think most of our problems lie in marketing, and Terry really did set us back a few quarters."

"What was the problem with Terry anyway?" Kathryn asked.

The directness of the question caused Andrew to shift in his chair. "Well, he wasn't able to move quickly enough in terms of revamping our advertising. It wasn't just his creative skills. He wasn't a very good manager either."

"Did you hire him?"

Andrew nodded.

"Then his failure is your responsibility."

Now the other board members squirmed a little.

"Did you look into his management skills when you hired him?"

Andrew stammered. "Well, sure, I mean, as much as you do with anyone. I mean, you figure he can manage if he's an executive. He came highly recommended."

Kathryn persisted. "What are you looking for in his replacement? How are you going to make sure you don't make the same mistake?"

Andrew couldn't really answer the question. Suddenly, a banging sound broke the tension. It seemed that someone outside the boardroom was pounding a nail into a wall. Joan rose from her seat and went outside to see what was happening.

The Chairman jumped in. "Okay, Kathryn. I think you've made a few good points. But this is a little too—" he searched for a word.

Stephen finished the sentence. "Unfair. I mean, it's easy for you to take shots at us like that when things aren't going too well, but it's not as simple as you make it sound. How are we supposed to know if a guy is going to tank like Terry did?"

The room went silent again. Until Janice joined in. "I'd have to agree. We did all we could, given the marketing situation. And we're not the only ones with this problem. Two of our competitors lost key executives last quarter. They're going to have the same problems that we did."

Other board members seemed to agree passively.

The pounding stopped, and Joan came back into the room.

Kathryn spoke again, but with a hint of sarcasm. "Well, maybe you're doing better than I thought." She seemed willing to let the conversation go with that remark.

Silence.

The Chairman spoke. "Okay. Good discussion. Let's call it—"

Andrew interrupted. "No. We're not doing better than you thought." He looked at Kathryn. "We've made too many mistakes. Terry was given no management support. We all saw him struggling and we just let it go on. *I* let it go on." The room froze. Slowly, Andrew pushed his chair away from the table and stood. All eyes were fixed upon him.

During the next ten minutes, Andrew delivered the speech of his life. He talked about results. He talked about accountability. He talked about clarity and conflict. He congratulated Kathryn on being willing to put the tough issues on the table.

"Maybe now we'll get clear on our real issues," he even said.

The Board was dumbfounded.

Before he finished, Andrew said, "And if we continue the way we're going now, if our results continue to slide, then I probably shouldn't be in this job. It's time that all of us became more accountable for the way things are around here. And it's going to start with me." He hoped he would not come to regret that remark.

Just as he finished, the pounding resumed out in the hallway.

The Chairman closed the meeting. "Alright. Thank you all for your energy and input. We'll see you in about twelve weeks." The board members gathered their things and headed for the door, with Andrew a few steps behind.

As the group moved across the hallway to the elevators, Andrew again became aware of the pounding sound. He looked over and saw a maintenance guy hanging a series of pictures along the hallway wall.

He asked Joan, "What's this all about?"

"We found some old pictures of past CEOs and thought they'd look nice here by the board room." Andrew nodded his approval and decided to go take a look at the photos. As the elevator doors opened, the Chairman asked, "Are you coming, Andrew?"

Distracted, he shook his head. "I'll see you downstairs."

Everyone but Andrew got into the elevator, and the doors closed.

Approaching the first photo, he saw that it was an old picture of himself without as much gray hair as he had now. Beneath the photo was Andrew's name and an empty space for an ending date.

The next three photos were Andrew's most recent pre-decessors, who had run the company for almost twenty-five years collectively. The next photo was a handsome man who looked familiar to Andrew but whom he couldn't place. The name below was not familiar at all, nor were the dates.

Andrew noted that the pounding stopped and the mainte-nance man, his back turned, was putting his hammer in his belt. His job seemed complete.

Turning back toward the black and white photos, Andrew recognized the face in the next one almost immediately. The Bald Man.

Andrew went back to the previous photo and now realized that it was the Stylish Man. He suspected that the third photo would be—yes, it was—the Tall Man.

Finally, the next photo was a kind-looking man with white hair and a wrinkled smile who could be no one but Charlie. "Charles Pierce," actually.

Suddenly it dawned on Andrew that the maintenance man was wearing the same color shirt that Charlie wore the night before in his dream. Turning toward the end of the hallway, Andrew saw the old man turn the corner.

He yelled, "Sir?! Charlie?!"

The old man did not answer or reappear. Andrew sprinted to the end of the hall, turned the corner, and saw no one.

Three Years Later

The board room was again crowded. The Chairman
began. "Well, it has been a terrific year, especially
considering the results of the prior two or three
years. The company is healthier than it has been in a
long time, our marketing is more assertive, our turnover
is down, and our revenue is growing again. The stock
price is high enough that we can even consider a midyear
split."

Golf applause from the board members.

Kathryn joined in. "I think the executive team deserves a
lot of credit. The decisiveness and discipline of leadership
here have been amazing."

Kathryn and the rest of the board turned toward their CEO, who could barely keep from smiling as he replied: "Thank you. I appreciate your kind words, but I don't deserve the credit. Certainly my team has been terrific. And the guidance of the board has been helpful."

The Chairman smiled knowingly to acknowledge the modesty.

The CEO then seemed to remember someone. "And ironically, I received some pretty good advice from an unlikely person."

The room was silent with curiosity.

The Chairman asked, "Who was that?"

"Andrew O'Brien," the CEO responded. The board members were surprised.

The Chairman spoke. "Andrew? How is he? I haven't talked to him since his last board meeting."

"You know, he seemed fine. But we didn't really talk about him."

Kathryn asked, "Where did you see him?"

"That's the funny thing," the CEO remarked with a smile. "I ran into him one night on a BART train."

AFTERWORD

AFTERWORD

All leaders struggle because, like Andrew, they are susceptible to one or more of the five temptations. But having those temptations is not why they ultimately *fail*. Leaders fail because they are unwilling to put their temptations on the table for others to see. For it is only by bringing their temptations into the open that leaders can enlist the support of subordinates who are in a unique position to help.

The trouble is that this calls for a seemingly excessive level of scrutiny, which many leaders resent and resist. They cannot understand why people in their organizations continue to monitor and comment on their behavior when there are so many other problems within the company that need fixing. Of course, they are missing the point entirely. What they perceive as criticism is actually invaluable counsel.

When I work with executive teams, I explain that if the CEO's behavior is ninety-five percent healthy while the rest of the organization is just fifty percent sound, I'll choose to focus on that crucial and leveraged five percent that makes up the remainder of the CEO's behavior.

Although every leader agrees in theory with this line of thinking, few are willing to put it into practice and endure the painful self-examination required to "fix" that final five percent. And yet, a willingness to do this is exactly what separates leaders who succeed from those who fail.

If this is so, then why don't all leaders endure the pain? Because too many of them mistakenly believe they can avoid it and still find a way to succeed. What they are doing is trading short-term pain (the struggle) for long-term pain (failure).

The key to success, then, is not to avoid the susceptibility to the five temptations. While that would be desirable, it is an impossibility. The key is to embrace the self-examination that reveals the temptations and to keep them in the open where they can be addressed.

Of course, this cannot be accomplished overnight; it cannot be wrapped in a tidy, happy ending in which our heroic CEO realizes his temptations and suddenly becomes the world's most effective leader. Like so much of life, it is a messy, constant, and unavoidable process, but one that great leaders welcome.

THE MODEL

THE MODEL

. . . . .

A Summary of Why Executives Fail

The greatest challenge of being a CEO, or any leader for that matter, is to avoid getting trapped by the daily complexities and details of our "business." To rise above that challenge, we must learn to embrace the five behaviors that Andrew and Charlie outlined in the fable. These behaviors are difficult to master not because they are complicated but because each presents us with a corresponding temptation, a natural tendency toward human frailty. Oddly enough, some of these temptations may not seem like frailties at all in our personal lives. That is the subject of a different discussion. But in our roles as leaders, the temptations are poison.

TEMPTATION 1

The most important principle that an executive must embrace is a desire to produce results. As obvious as this sounds, it is not universally practiced by the highest-ranking executives in many companies. Many CEOs put something ahead of results on their list of priorities, and it represents the most dangerous of all the temptations: the desire to protect the status of their careers.

How can a person become the CEO of a company and not be a maniac for results? Most CEOs *were* results maniacs before reaching their ultimate jobs. Once they "arrive," though, many of them focus primarily on preserving their status. This occurs because their real purpose in life has always been personal gain. With nowhere to go but down, it almost makes sense that once they have achieved their ultimate status, they will do whatever they can to protect it.

This causes CEOs to make decisions that protect their ego or reputation or, worse yet, to avoid making decisions that might damage them. They reward people who contribute to their ego, instead of those who contribute to the results of the company.

This poses a good question: Don't executives realize that by focusing on results they will ultimately achieve greater status and ego satisfaction in their careers? Yes, but this requires a lot of work over a long period of time. It allows for too many risky episodes of status-loss along the way. Remember, even temporary loss of status is unacceptable to CEOs who do not resist this temptation.

Simple advice for CEOs: make results the most important measure of personal success, or step down from the job. The future of the company you lead is too important for customers, employees, and stockholders to hold it hostage to your ego.

TEMPTATION 2

Even CEOs who resist the temptation to overfocus on protecting their status sometimes fail. Why? Because they do not hold their direct reports accountable for delivering on the commitments that drive results. This happens because they succumb to a different temptation: the desire to be popular.

Wanting to be well liked by peers is an understandable, but dangerous, problem for CEOs. Being at the top of an organization is lonely. There are very few people in a company with whom CEOs spend considerable time, aside from their direct reports.

Those reports are often the same age and earn the same

kind of money as the CEO, especially relative to other employees in the company. Most CEOs become friends with their reports and commiserate about the constant needs and shortfalls of employees. They develop a sense of camaraderie around their overwhelming responsibilities. It is no surprise, then, that when it comes time for a CEO to tell these same people that they are not meeting expectations, they balk.

Empirical evidence of this phenomenon is that CEOs conduct performance reviews for their direct reports far less diligently than do managers at other levels. Why? It isn't because they are too busy or lazy, but because they don't want to deal with the prospect of upsetting one of their peers. Ironically, those same CEOs will not hesitate to ultimately fire a direct report when his or her performance problem becomes too costly, thereby severing the relationship completely. But they often fail to provide constructive or negative feedback along the way.

Simple advice for CEOs: work for the long-term respect of your direct reports, not for their affection. Don't view them as a support group, but as key employees who must deliver on their commitments if the company is to produce predictable results. And remember, your people aren't going to like you anyway if they ultimately fail.

TEMPTATION 3

Even CEOs who resist the temptation to protect their status and to be popular with their direct reports sometimes fail. Why? Because even if they are *willing* to hold their direct reports accountable, they are often reluctant to do so because they don't think it's fair. That's because they haven't made it clear what those direct reports are accountable for doing. Why don't they make these things clear? Because they give in to yet another temptation: the need to make "correct" decisions, to achieve certainty.

Many CEOs, especially highly analytical ones, want to ensure that their decisions are correct, which is impossible in a world of imperfect information and uncertainty. Still, executives with a need for precision and correctness often postpone decisions and fail to make their people's deliverables clear. They provide vague and hesitant direction to their direct reports and hope that they figure out the right answers along the way. The chances that they will produce the results CEOs eventually decide they want are slim.

Simple advice for CEOs: make clarity more important than accuracy. Remember that your people will learn more if you take decisive action than if you always wait for more information. And if the decisions you make in the spirit of creating clarity turn out to be wrong when more information becomes available, change plans and explain why. It is your job to risk being wrong. The only real cost to you of being wrong is loss of pride. The cost to your company of not taking the risk of being wrong is paralysis.

TEMPTATION 4

Even CEOs who resist the temptation to protect their status, to be popular with their direct reports, and to make correct decisions sometimes fail because they don't feel comfortable with the decisions they make. That's because they haven't benefited from the best sources of information that are always available to them: their direct reports. Why not? Because they give in to the next temptation: the desire for harmony.

Most people, including CEOs, believe that it is better for people to agree and get along than disagree and conflict with one another. That is how they are raised. However, harmony sometimes restricts "productive ideological conflict," the passionate interchange of opinions around an issue.

Without this kind of conflict, decisions are often suboptimal. The best decisions are made only after all knowledge and perspectives are out on the table. Not every person's perspective and opinion can be agreed with, but they can be considered. When all available knowledge is considered, the chances of optimal decisions are greater—not to mention the likelihood of confidence in those decisions, which is just as important.

Simple advice for CEOs: tolerate discord. Encourage your direct reports to air their ideological differences, and with passion. Tumultuous meetings are often signs of progress. Tame ones are often signs of leaving important issues off the table. Guard against personal attacks, but not to the point of stifling important interchanges of ideas.

TEMPTATION 5

Even CEOs who resist the temptation to protect their status, to be popular with their direct reports, to make correct decisions, and to create harmony sometimes fail. Why? Because even though *they* are willing to cultivate productive conflict, *their people* may not be willing to do so. Why not? Because the CEO gives in to the final temptation: the desire for invulnerability.

CEOs are relatively powerful people. Being vulnerable with their peers and reports is not a comfortable prospect. They mistakenly believe that they lose credibility if their people feel too comfortable challenging their ideas.

No matter how much these CEOs encourage productive conflict, they do not achieve it because it doesn't feel safe to their people, who see them as unwilling to enter the fray. As a result, those reports position themselves around the inferred opinion of the CEO and conflict with one another only when it is politically expedient.

Simple advice for CEOs: actively encourage your people to challenge your ideas. Trust them with your reputation and your ego. As a CEO, this is the greatest level of trust that you can give. They will return it with respect and honesty, and with a desire to be vulnerable among their peers.

CEOs who focus on results more than status, accountability more than popularity, clarity more than certainty, productive conflict more than harmony, and trust more than invulnerability can still fail, but only if they are thwarted by competitive and market pressures that are largely out of their control.

The model, on page 119, is displayed in seemingly reverse order to show the sequential impact of the principles on one another. Instilling trust gives executives the confidence to have productive conflict. Fostering conflict gives executives confidence to create clarity. Clarity gives executives the confidence to hold people accountable. Accountability gives executives confidence in expected results. And results are a CEO's ultimate measure of long-term success.

Overcoming the Five Temptations

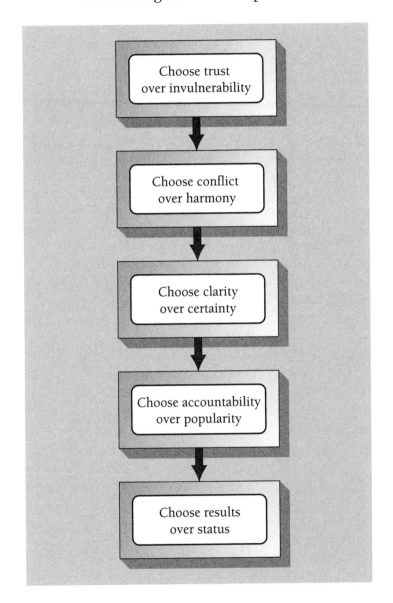

PART
. . . . .
4

SELF-ASSESSMENT

Self-Assessment

Ultimately, the best way to understand which of the five temptations is most tempting to you is to simply reflect on the model and decide which temptations seem to fit. A good way to do this is to ask yourself, "Which of the temptations made me feel uncomfortable?" Although this is certainly unscientific, the best self-assessment is often unstructured and qualitative.

However, some people prefer to use a diagnostic tool to provide a little structure in the search for their temptation(s). One such tool is provided here.

Some of the questions are tricky in that they do not seem to reveal weaknesses at all. However, keep in mind that this tool is designed to identify your *susceptibility* to a given temptation, not to determine that you definitely succumb to it. Ultimately, this has to be your call.

TEMPTATION 1
Choosing status over results

- Do you personally consider it a professional failure when your organization fails to meet its objectives?

- Do you often wonder, *What's next? What will I do to top this in my career?*

- Would it bother you greatly if your company exceeded its objectives but you remained somewhat anonymous relative to your peers in the industry?

Rationale

On a professional level, organizational success and personal-professional success are one and the same. Although it is healthy for any human being to separate his or her sense of self-esteem from success on the job, in the context of professional success these should not be divided. Too often, CEOs justify their own performance even when the organizations they lead are failing around them.

CEOs must ultimately judge their personal-professional success by the results on the bottom line. This is not to suggest that other "human" factors are not important, or even most important on a spiritual and emotional level. However, only the CEO is ultimately responsible for the results of the company, and this must be his or her final measure.

Additionally, a pronounced concern for the "next step" in a person's career is a good sign of susceptibility to Temptation Number One because it is a possible indication that success is being gauged in terms of career advancement rather than current performance. The most successful CEOs focus almost exclusively on their current jobs.

Finally, worrying about how much public recognition one receives is a possible sign of susceptibility to the first Temptation. Although human nature dictates that we hope for a just share of acknowledgment, it is a dangerous part of human nature to entertain. Certainly, at one time or another all CEOs have experienced short shrift when it comes to public recognition. Those who eventually get that recognition are the CEOs who aren't distracted by the occasional slighting that an unscientific press is sure to give. Interestingly enough, they experience a low degree of satisfaction from such press. After all, they take larger personal satisfaction from achieving results.

TEMPTATION 2
Choosing popularity over accountability

- Do you consider yourself to be a close friend of your direct reports?

- Does it bother you to the point of distraction if they are unhappy with you?

- Do you often find yourself reluctant to give negative feedback to your direct reports? Do you water down negative feedback to make it more palatable?

- Do you often vent to them about issues in the organization? For example, do you refer to your staff as "we" and other employees as "they"?

Rationale

It is wonderful for CEOs to care about direct reports as people, so long as they can separate the success of those relationships from their sense of self-esteem and personal happiness. This is difficult because most of us try to avoid major disagreements with close friends, and it is impossible not to be concerned about a deep rift with one of them. If those close friends are your direct reports, the accountability within the organization can be threatened. The slightest reluctance to hold someone accountable for their behaviors and results can cause an avalanche of negative reaction from others who perceive even the slightest hint of unfairness or favoritism.

Those CEOs who are able to make close friendships with direct reports and still avoid a sense of favoritism often find it easy to use those reports as their personal "venting boards." All executives need people they can vent to about challenges they face in the organization (for example, people they are frustrated with), but CEOs must resist the desire to use direct reports for this service. It can lead to politics among the executive team, and more importantly, it can undermine the team's objective understanding of their own actions by creating an atmosphere of self-victimizing groupthink. Often this manifests itself during executive staff meetings in comments such as "When will these people stop questioning us and start understanding what we are trying to do?"

TEMPTATION 3
Choosing certainty over clarity

- Do you pride yourself on being intellectually precise?
- Do you prefer to wait for more information rather than make a decision without all of the facts?
- Do you enjoy debating details with your direct reports during meetings?

Rationale
Certainly, intellectual precision alone is not a sign of Temptation Number Three. However, when it manifests

itself during staff meetings in terms of unnecessary debates over minutiae, it is a sign of real trouble.

It is no surprise that many CEOs take a great deal of pride in their analytical and intellectual acumen. Unable to realize that their success as an executive usually has less to do with intellectual skills than it does with personal and behavioral discipline, they spend too much time debating the finer points of decision making. Those debates are problematic for two reasons. First, they eat up valuable time that can be spent discussing larger issues, which often receive just a few minutes at the end of the staff meeting agenda. Second, and more important, they create a climate of excessive analysis and overintellectualization of tactical issues. If there is one person in an organization who cannot afford to be *overly* precise, it is the CEO.

TEMPTATION 4

Choosing harmony over productive conflict

- Do you prefer your meetings to be pleasant and enjoyable?
- Are your meetings often boring?
- Do you get uncomfortable at meetings if your direct reports argue?

- Do you often make peace or try to reconcile direct reports who are at odds with one another?

Rationale

Executives often bemoan the number of meetings they attend, and they include staff meetings with their peers at the top of that list. They often complain about meetings taking up time that is needed for "real work." This is a good sign that those meetings are not as difficult (that is, are not as productive) as they should be.

Productive executive staff meetings should be exhausting inasmuch as they are passionate, critical discussions. Pleasant meetings—or even worse, boring ones—are indications that there is not a proper level of overt, constructive, ideological conflict taking place. But don't be deceived. *Every* meeting has conflict. Some executives just sweep that conflict under the table and let employees deeper in the organization sort it out. This doesn't happen by accident.

When executives do get into an issue, CEOs often squelch any potential for passion by making peace. This sends a message that pleasant, agreeable meetings are preferred by the CEO. After a few pleasant meetings, boredom sets in and executives start lamenting the real work they could be doing.

TEMPTATION 5
Choosing invulnerability over trust

- Do you have a hard time admitting when you're wrong?
- Do you fear that your direct reports want your job?
- Do you try to keep your greatest weaknesses secret from your direct reports?

Rationale

No one loves to admit being wrong, but some people hate it. Great CEOs don't lose face in the slightest when they are wrong, because they know who they are, they know why they are the CEO, and they realize that the organization's results, not the appearance of being smart, are their ultimate measure of success. They know that the best way to get results is to put their weaknesses on the table and invite people to help them minimize those weaknesses. CEOs who understand this concept intellectually but cannot behavioralize it sometimes make the mistake of finding symbolic moments to admit mistakes and weaknesses. This only serves to reinforce the notion that the CEO is unwilling to put real weaknesses on the table. Overcoming this temptation requires a degree of fear and pain that many CEOs are unwilling to tolerate.

If you have a difficult time identifying your temptations, you may want to ask your direct reports to answer the questions above and compare your responses to theirs.

Acknowledgments

First, thanks to my wife for her love and counsel and to the rest of my family for their constant support.

Thanks also to Amy Adair for her selfless efforts to organize me and to keep me on top of this book while we were starting a business; to Susan Williams for understanding exactly what Andrew and Charlie were trying to say, and for having passion about it; to my amazing staff at The Table Group for their many suggestions and ideas; to the numerous clients, colleagues, and friends who have given me encouragement over the years, especially Joel Mena, Sally DeStefano, and Gary Bolles; and to the entire team at Jossey-Bass for their commitment to bringing this together.

A special thanks to all the CEOs and other executives I've worked with who taught me how simple yet difficult it is to be a leader and who helped lead me toward the realization of the Five Temptations.

And most important, thanks to God for everything I have and am.

About the Author

Patrick Lencioni is founder and president of The Table Group, a management consulting firm specializing in executive team development and organizational health. As a consultant and keynote speaker, he has worked with thousands of senior executives in organizations ranging from Fortune 500s and high-tech start-ups to universities and nonprofits. Clients who have engaged his services include Southwest Airlines, General Mills, Microsoft, New York Life, Cox Communications, Allstate, Visa, FedEx, and the U.S. Military Academy, West Point, to name a few. He is the author of seven nationally recognized books, including the *New York Times* best-seller *The Five Dysfunctions of a Team* (Jossey-Bass, 2002).

Patrick lives in the San Francisco Bay Area with his wife, Laura, and their four sons, Matthew, Connor, Casey, and Michael.

To learn more about Patrick and The Table Group, please visit www.tablegroup.com.

To learn more about Patrick Lencioni and his
other products and services, including free
resources and his newsletter, please visit
www.tablegroup.com

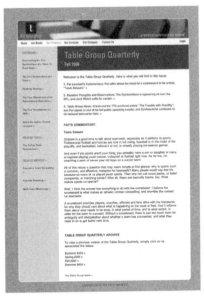

Newsletter

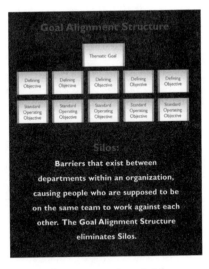

Silos Downloadable
Tool

the table group